What the **Bible** Really Says about **Women**

What the **Bible** Really Says about **Women**

Sheri Adams

Smyth & Helwys Publishing, Inc.
Macon, Georgia

ISBN 1-880837-88-9

What the Bible Really Says about Women
by Sheri Adams

The paper used in this publication meets the minimum
requirements of American Standard for Information
Sciences—Permanence of paper for Printed Library
Materials, ANSI Z39.48–1984.

Library of Congress Cataloging-in-Publication Data

Adams, Sheri.
    What the Bible really says about women / Sheri
Adams.
    x + pp.   6 x 9" (15 x 23 cm.)
    ISBN 1-880837-88-9
    1. Bible—Feminist criticism. 2. Women in the Bible.
3. Jesus Christ—Views on women. 4. Women in Chris-
tianity—History—Early church, ca. 60–300. I. Title.
    BS521.4.A335   1994
    220.8'3054—dc20   94-28
                                          CIP

Contents

Preface

This book has grown out of a class that I developed and taught at the International Baptist Theological Seminary in Buenos Aires, Argentina. Those students inherited the same interpretations and traditions that have prevented women from fully exercising their gifts in the church for centuries. I hoped to speak to the question of women in ministry in Argentina by demonstrating that the Bible has more to say than a particular interpretation of three or four passages.

My understanding of war and the Jubilee in the Old Testament has been formed largely by the writings of some Mennonites, especially John Howard Yoder. I am indebted to the works of Fisher Humphreys and Frank Stagg for my theology in general. I hardly know any more if I think their thoughts or mine. Those persons familiar with Evelyn and Frank Stagg's book, *Woman in the World of Jesus*, will recognize it as a resource in the development of this material. The hermeneutical tool in chapter 1 came from my husband, who got it in seed form in seminary in the 1950s and has worked with it through the years.

Part of what I have written has grown out of my own personal Bible reading and study. For ten years I have set a goal to read all the Bible during the year. A few times— due to parental, work, or church responsibilities—I have not finished, but the following year I have forgiven myself and started again. I am a better teacher because of it and, I hope, a better Christian.

Sheri Adams
Buenos Aires, Argentina

To my parents

William Flinn Dawson

and

Effie Sharkey Dawson

with love and thanks

Chapter 1

The Bible

To understand what the Bible says about women or any other theme, we first need to try to understand the Bible itself. We often think that the Bible is eternal as God is eternal, that somehow it came into our hands completely formed as it is now, and that all we have to do is read it and we will understand it. It helps us understand the Bible more as we read and study, however, if we have some idea of how the Bible developed. Try to imagine the time when the Bible as we know it did not exist. We know that Adam and Eve had no Bible; neither did Noah nor the partriarchs. As the art of writing developed, much of the material that had been passed along in oral form was recorded and the Bible in written form began its long development.

The Development of the Bible

Israel understood itself to have a unique relationship with God. God had called its ancestors, Abraham and Sarah, who had responded positively in faith. God had made a covenant with them; they were elected. God worked through Abraham and Sarah and their descendents to form the nation, Israel. The people of Israel understood this election by God to have significance in their everyday lives, that is to say, in history. It was through the nation's history that Israel came to understand God and God's will. The written record of this understanding in light of history is part of what the Bible is and is also the background from which the theology and ethics of Israel grew.

Two major historical events of the Old Testament shaped Israel's understanding of God—and thus also shaped its theology and ethics. One was the exodus; the other was the fall of Jerusalem around 586 B.C.. The exodus was more than liberation from Egyptian slavery, though it certainly included that. Exodus was a call and response, the formation of a people, the giving of a land in which to live, the giving of commandments to govern the new society. All of this was involved in covenant, in election.

A logical question to ask, and one that the people of the new nation did ask, was, "Why did God elect us out of all the peoples of the world? We are not the biggest nor the strongest. Then, why? Why us?" The answer that they themselves gave was that God had elected them to be a light to the world. They were to shine in the darkness as the city on a hill of which Jesus spoke, pointing the way to God in much the same way that the lights from the city directed the night traveler.

Once it was clear to the Israelites that they were to be God's earthly light, they asked themselves, "How do we do this?" They came to understand that they were to share God's message with their neighbors, to be missionaries. The next step was to understand the message, itself. Israel increasingly realized as it lived out its history as God's people that God's message touched every aspect of life.

Too often as the church, as God's people this side of history, we focus only on the theology Israel had to share. To call attention to the ethical aspects of the message is not an attempt to diminish the importance of the theology, which in its day was unique, but to stress that theology was only part of the message. God was interested in theology and straightened out a misconception of the day: Gods and goddesses that behaved like decadent human beings did not exist in heaven; only one god was there. God also insisted, contrary to the popular theology of the day, that God was moral and just and concerned that people also be moral and just.

The laws that God gave helped people understand God's ethics. God's laws mirrored God's concerns. For instance, the law reflected God's concern that people learn to relate both to God and to one another. The law demonstrated God's concern for quality of life, both for the individual and the community. God was concerned with the very survival of Israel and told the people that some foods were clean and therefore edible, and that some were unclean and not to be eaten. We do not claim to understand all that was involved in the giving of this law concerning clean and unclean foods, but we can see from our present-day perspective that the unclean foods were those that would spoil quickly, especially in a desert climate.

The law dealt with the treatment of the sick, and God taught the people the use of the quarantine—not only of people but of houses, clothing, and other items. The law dealt with the sanitary conditions of the camps and towns where the people lived. God taught the people to put the latrines outside the camps and towns and to wash their hands after relieving themselves and after touching dead or dirty things, animals, or people. When we consider that the laws were given thousands of years before germs were discovered, the only explanation for what we have in the Bible is direct revelation from God. The society that practiced or kept these laws would enjoy better health and longer life.

The law, however, touched more than these survival techniques. The law dealt with rights—human rights. Under the law, all people had rights—even widows, orphans, strangers, and slaves. These were the weak and defenseless people of the society, those completely dependent on the goodwill of other people, those who —as a rule were taken advantage of by others.

The law was concerned with family relationships: fathers and mothers were to be honored; husbands and wives were to be faithful to one another; a husband did not have the right simply to throw his wife out if he so chose—he was required to give her a bill of divorce, which freed her from her obligations to him and recognized her right to remarry and rebuild her life.

The law prohibited theft, murder, false witness, and covetousness because there must be some measure of trust for the society to function. These laws reflect God's concern for stable societies.

One of the most interesting and revealing parts of the law is the concept of the Jubilee and all that it implied, including economic justice from God's point of view. Most of the Jubilee concepts are spelled out in Leviticus 25, although Jubilee ethics and theology lie behind other Old Testament passages. Probably the most distinguishing feature of the Jubilee was the concept of a tribe's land as an eternal possession. Land, like people, could be bought and sold but only for fifty years at a time.

Jubilee ethics required that debts be canceled, slaves be freed, and the land lie fallow every seven years. Every forty-nine years the land was to enjoy a double sabbath, which basically meant no agricultural work for the people for two years. No wonder they were told to proclaim liberty throughout the land!

It is easy to see that the practice of Jubilee ethics was a powerful testimony. A tremendous act of faith would have been required to plant no crops, depending completely on God's promise to provide. Neighbors surely would have asked about this strange and dangerous practice. The inability to sell the family's inheritance permanently, the canceling of debts, and the freeing of slaves gave these people a distinctive economic structure. The obvious result was that although a family could fall on hard times and become poor, it could never permanently lose the means to support itself. A new start came every fifty years.

The flip side, of course, is that every fifty years the rich were more or less back to square one. Under this system it was not impossible to get rich, but it certainly was not easy. It was not impossible to exploit the poor, but there was a limit to how long the same people could be exploited. To make things even more difficult for the rich, they were prohibited by God from charging interest on money lent. Under this system it seemed useless to waste all one's energies simply trying to accumulate more and more; and, if one did not spend his or her energies that way, he or she would have time for other things—God, family, and self. *(Fool* is the word the Bible uses for the person who spends all of life's time and energies storing up this world's treasures.)

Jubilee concepts help us to understand Jesus better. When his disciples rebuked the woman for anointing Jesus' feet with the expensive perfume, which could have been sold and given to the poor, Jesus said: "The poor you will have with you always" (Matt 26:11). This is a direct quotation of Deuteronomy 15:11, but it cannot be understood apart from its context. Deuteronomy

15:1-11 telescopes a range of historical experiences regarding the poor into a brief statement that shows a progression from the conditional promise that there be no poor ("if only"), to instructions on how to treat the poor, to the realization that disobedience of the conditional promise has resulted in poverty as a permanent reality.

Jesus was not saying that we must resign ourselves to the fact that we will always have poor people and that nothing can be done about it. He was saying that we will always have poor people because we are not willing to put God's economics into practice. Jesus was not trying to comfort his disciples; he was condemning them. A hypothesis in New Testament studies implies that one of the reasons the Jews of Jesus' day rejected him as Messiah was that he was calling them to practice once again the Jubilee, and that they, especially the Saduccees and wealthy Pharisees, had too much to lose in terms of properties and riches.

Many scholars believe the Israelites never practiced the Jubilee, at least not fully or for long. Israel did understand the Jubilee to be God's will, however, and that the refusal to honor it was one of the reaons for Israel's hardships. The Israelites lost their land and liberty and suffered seventy years in exile. They had to understand their losses and suffering in light of the fact that they were God's chosen people. Why had God allowed God's people to suffer so?

The answer that they themselves gave after a time of reflection was: We sinned. We did not obey God's laws. We intermarried with strangers. We worshiped other gods; we even sacrificed our children—God's children—to these foreign gods. We worshiped the sun, the moon, the stars—God's creations instead of the Creator. The loss of Jerusalem, the loss of the land, and the suffering of exile were our punishments for disobeying God. Actually God, being merciful, punished us less than we deserved.

Out of all of this history, this reflection, this life, came the idea of "next time." The Hebrews promised: Next time we will obey God. Next time we will love our neighbors. Next time we will practice the Jubilee. Next time we will surely do a better job of being God's light.

Our question now is how to relate the Bible to all of this history? The Bible—first the Old Testament and later the New—grew and developed from the life of Israel and later from the life of the early church with all of their strengths and weaknesses, virtues and sins. The Bible was not written in a vacuum. From reading the Old Testament, for instance, we see that a body of literature was available to aid in the preparation of the books we now have. At first, much of what later came to be written down survived in oral form, poetry, genealogies, and admonitions of the prophets. We assume that some, if not most, of the oral tradition was later recorded.

We do not, however, have all of these early writings. For instance, in several places in Samuel and Kings we read about books of the kings, one for the kings of Israel and one for those in Judah. 2 Kings 14:28 refers to the northern version as the Book of the Chronicles of the Kings of Israel. The writers of Samuel, Kings, and the biblical books of Chronicles chose not to use all of the information available in the other books about the kings. We do not have any of those books. Nor do we have the other books about the Hebrew kings mentioned in the Bible. We do not have any of the three books containing David's acts referred to in 1 Chronicles 29:29, though they may be the sources behind some of the accounts we do have. We do not have a book called The Books of the Wars of the Lord (Num 21:14), nor do we have the books mentioned in Joshua 18:9, 2 Samuel 1:18, and 1 Samuel 10:25. Neither do we have any rationale by which we can explain why God preserved for us the books we have and not these others.

The same is true of the New Testament. We have only part of the correspondence between Paul and the Corinthian church, for instance. We do not have a letter from Laodicea that is mentioned in Colossians 4:16. We simply trust God that what we need was preserved.

We also know that the other nations of the day produced works of literature in which the authors grappled with some of the same themes as did the writers of the Bible: Who created the world, for instance? What are the rights of the different classes of human beings? Where does one find the meaning of life? Reading the Bible in the light of the literature of its day, we can see that the Bible offers us an interpretation of life filtered through faith in this particular God and in God's demands on our lives. If one's faith was in a different god of the day, a different interpretation of life was offered. Thus it is in in our society, even within the body of faith, that people do not always see things exactly the same way. We may have two or three different opinions, different ways of understanding, different points of view, different points of emphasis. So did people of biblical times. This helps us see, for instance, why we have in the Bible three accounts of creation.

The passages dealing with Noah and the preparation for the flood are also good examples of writing from distinct perspective. In one account the emphasis is apparently on God's concern to preserve all species of life; thus Noah was directed to take two animals— one male, one female—of each type. In another account the emphasis is on the provision for sacrifices after the flood. Noah was instructed to take two of the unclean animals and seven of the clean animals, which would provide him with the necessary sacrifices when the time came.

Consider also the way in which the authors of the Kings materials and the authors of the Chronicles materials presented the life of King David. Chronicles contains no mention of David's adultery, of the problems within the royal family, nor anything about the struggle for power—both within and outside the family —at the end of David's life. There is no reason to think that the author tried to hide these facts from his readers, for they are available in other sources. The author simply had other purposes in mind.

We do not always understand God's will perfectly; we struggle to understand. Much of our theological reflection is the attempt to understand God and God's will for us and to explain it in terms that we can comprehend. So it was for the Israelites. They asked: What is God's ideal will for our nation? Is it that we have a holy line of priests, or is it that all the people are holy? In Numbers 16 a man named Korah and others dared to suggest to Moses that all the congregation might be holy; and they, their wives, their sons, and their little ones paid for that theology with their lives.

This suggestion did not answer the questions. Next the people struggled with the issue of whether a person suffers for his or her sins only, or whether a person suffers for the sins for his or her parents, also. The entire chapter of Ezekiel 18 is a theological treatise on this problem.

Sometimes, even when God had actually done something on their behalf, the Israelites looked back over a period of history and did not completely understand what God had intended. A good example of this is seen in the giving, taking, and settling of the promised land. Since we find differing boundary lines in different parts of the Old Testament, it seems fair to say that there were different interpretations of just how much land God had actually given to them.

They also differed in their understandings of how God had actually given them the land. Did God alone do something that resulted in emptying the land so that the people could simply move in, live in cities they had not built, and eat of vineyards they had not planted? Or was God's method of taking the land a kind of holy war in which they had to participate?

Even after most of the land had been taken, many of the original inhabitants still lived in the land with the Israelites. Many Israelites were confused about this; they had understood that the land would be theirs alone. Were the original inhabitants still there because the Israelites could not expel them or because they did not expel them, or were they there so God could teach the next generation of Israelites war? (See Josh 15:63; 13:13; 16:10; Judg 3:1–2.)

Modern-day writers on religious subjects find that they often return to a former piece of writing and revise it or use parts of it while adding some additional mate-rial. The themes of the Bible are timeless; often all that is needed is to bring the same message up to date. Sometimes writers even update the timeless message of some other writer. For instance, in the 1970s, H. H. Hobbs updated the still valuable book of E. Y. Mullins, *The Axioms of Religion*, which was written in the 1920s. Evidence of later revision of older texts is found in the many editoral notes scattered throughout the Old Testament. (See Gen. 36:31 or Josh 13:13.)

Just as the world of our day affects how we think, how we express ourselves, and what we do, the world of their day affected the writers of the Bible. We must account for this in any theory of inspiration that we devise. The same man, Paul, wrote Galatians 3:26–28 and Colossians 3:11. It seems fair to ask if there might have been some reason that he decided not to include the phrase about equality between men and women in Christ in the passage in Colossians. Other examples of the effects of the world on the biblical writers are passages like 2 Peter 2:4–9, 1 Peter 3:19, and Jude 9 and 14. One satisfactory way to understand them is to say that the New Testament writers had sources or traditions outside the Old Testament that we do not have and that their theology was affected by these additional sources.

In our day, Christians are often more comfortable with other Christians who are like them or who have some or many of the same concerns that they have. We have groups of Christians interested in peace and justice, for instance, or we have churches in which the majority of the people express similar theology. So it was for the early generations of God's people. It seems fair to say that some of the New Testament books grew out of different communities of faith; and, while all expressed belief in Jesus as savior, they may have differed on some things—like how much freedom should be given to slaves or women. The result is a New Testament that shows women, for instance, enjoying varying degrees of freedom within the church at different times and different places.

It is also important to take seriously the fact that God's people in early times had, as we have, only a part of the whole. The Bible itself tells us that we can only know in part, that God feels no obligation to reveal everything to us. (See Deut 29:29; Eccl 3:11.) We should not, however, be discouraged by our limitations. We have what we need. We need only the courage to read and believe and interpret what we have.

The Interpretation of the Bible

Much courage is needed to interpret the Bible, and I am convinced that most of the courage we need will come from simply reading and rereading all of the Bible until we feel we can speak of the Bible "as a whole." It is especially important when dealing with what the Bible has to say about women, not to read all the Bible by the light of two or three passages, but to read two or three passages by the light of the whole Bible.

The following is a tool that can help a person interpret the Bible. I take no claim for its originality, but I have often found it useful. Sometimes every part of the formula will be applicable to the passage in question; at other times one or several aspects of the formula will be useful. The idea is to ask, again to the extent that it is helpful, three questions of the passage and/or to apply one or two statements to the text.

The first question is: In this passage, does God speak, give a commandment, reveal something of God's nature and purpose, or do something? The point is, does God take the initiative? Divine initiative? Or is what we see the reaction of a human being or beings to something that God has done or said or revealed? Human response? Does the passage deal with the initiative of God or with human reaction?

Here are some examples. God took the initiative in calling Moses to the top of the mountain to give him the Ten Commandments. Moses responded positively by going to meet God and receive the commandments. After David's great sins of adultery and murder, God took the initiative of confronting him with his sin by sending the prophet, Nathan. David responded positively by confessing his sin. God took the initiative and called Jonah to go and warn the people of Ninevah of God's judgment. Jonah responded negatively by trying to run away. Jesus asked his disciples, "Who do the people think I am?" Peter responded positively by affirming that Jesus was the Christ. He then immediately responded negatively by refusing to consider the possibility that the Christ might suffer.

If we decide that in the passage at hand we have not a human response but the initiative of God, we ask another question, a question that is particularly helpful to ask of the words of God found in the Bible: When God speaks, is God telling us how things must be? If so, we call the passage a prescriptive passage. Or could it be that in the passage the words of God are not prescriptive but only descriptive? God is not telling us how things must be, but rather only describing how things are. There is an important difference. We spoke before of the link between the story of Jesus in Matthew 26:6–11 and Deuteronomy 15:1–11. In most sermons the words of Jesus concerning the permanent presence of the poor are interpreted as prescriptive, almost as if God wills that there be poor people, certainly as though nothing can be done about it. From reading Deuteronomy, however, we see that Jesus' words in Matthew are not prescriptive at all. They are descriptive, as are the words of God in Deuteronomy. God and, later,

Jesus are describing how things will be when God's people will not practice God's economy.

Sometimes the words of God in the Bible are prescriptive. When they clearly are, there is another question to ask. Did God intend that these words or this law be binding on all peoples, at all times, and in all places? If the answer to the question is yes, the words or the commandments are universal. God's will is that it never be changed.

Sometimes it is clear, however, that God did not intend for the law to be permanently binding on all people through all time. If this is the case, then the law is said to be particular—intended for this people, in this time, in this place. The dietary laws that we find in the Old Testament are good examples of laws that are particular. In fact, God makes it clear, in the rooftop visitation to Peter (Acts 10:9–16), that the laws prohibiting the eating of certain foods are canceled. The Ten Commandments are good examples of universal laws.

The fourth part of this tool for interpreting the Bible is not a question, but rather simply an observation. It is to note that, while the Christian life does have rules and goals to govern it, these rules and goals must never be cut loose from the personal relationship that we have with God through faith in Jesus Christ. We understand better as we live our faith that God did not give us rules to make us miserable or to prevent the enjoyment of life, but to protect us and to strengthen our relationship with God and with our fellow human beings. Basically we can say that the rules we find in the Bible are the rules of any good parent, rules that help the child grow as painlessly as possible to maturity, ones that serve as guides in any situation. Our goal in the Christian life is perfection. We, of course, never reach it. God forgives us; we try again. Through years of trying, we learn not to do and say some things and to do and say and think some other things and, in so doing, grow somewhat more Christlike.

The final part of the tool is to interpret the Bible in the light of Jesus Christ or by the light of the Gospels or to read the more difficult passages by the light of the passages that are easier to understand. This means that when we read Psalm 137:9—which says, "Happy shall he be who takes your little ones and dashes them against the rocks," which is probably a description of the way in which the infants of the foes were killed—we should understand that in no way can this verse represent God's will. We understand it in light of Jesus' words to love one's enemies and to do good to those who hate you in Matthew 5:43–44.

In summary, the questions for interpreting the Bible are:

(1) Does the passage in question speak to us of divine initiative or human response?

(2) If it is divine initiative, is it prescriptive or descriptive?

(3) If it is prescriptive, is it universal or particular?

The principles for applying them are:

(1) The rules and goals for the Christian life should be understood in light of our relationship with God through faith in Jesus Christ.

(2) We should read the Bible in the light of Jesus Christ.

I want to apply the tool to the Bible again, but this time I want to choose passages that help us with our task of understanding what the Bible has to teach about women.

1. Divine Initiative or human response?

Genesis 1:26–28 must be the passage par excellence for speaking of God's initiative and women. God created man and woman in God's image in one act of creation and gave them both equal responsibilities and privileges. We will return to this passage several times in our study because we have so much to learn from it.

2. Prescription or description?

In Genesis 3:14–19 we find the words of God to the serpent, the woman, and the man after they were confronted with and confessed their sin. It is fairly easy to interpret the words of God to the serpent and to the man as descriptive, for the passages read with a definite descriptive tone. It is not as easy to interpret the words of God to the woman as descriptive because they sound so prescriptive. "I will greatly multiply your pain in childbearing." This statement has a definite prescriptive ring. Yet, this is one of those times that the interpreter must have the courage of his or her convictions, after trying to understand the passage in light of the whole Bible, and say that, even though the passage sounds prescriptive, it is actually descriptive. God is describing the world of human relationships when men and women choose not to obey God's commandments.

These words from God to woman have been interpreted as prescriptive for centuries—so much so that, when anesthesia was developed and began to be used in childbirth, many conservative pastors and church leaders objected. They argued that it was God's will that women suffer in childbirth. To relieve that suffering was tampering with God's will. This theology did not prevail. The larger Christian community believed that God was more merciful than that.

Reading the Bible by the light of Jesus may be helpful here if we can mix two of the tools together. Jesus' words in Matthew 24:15–19 are interesting. He spoke about the inevitable war with Rome and how women, especially mothers, would suffer during that time. Jesus was observant; he paid attention. He noticed that pregnant women cannot run very fast; neither can a woman with a fifteen pound child in her arms. In times of crisis no one pays much attention to the young and the helpless, so they often suffer more.

Giving birth and having babies and young children to care for puts a woman at risk—and not only in times of war and crisis. Women do die in childbirth sometimes. Women do pay a price in personal freedom to care for the world's young; and, yet, in spite of the risks and the loss of personal freedom, the majority of women still want to marry and have a family. The point is that the woman puts herself in an unenviable situation because she wants to.

3. Universal or particular?

The two passages that come immediately to mind when thinking of universal or particular commandments are 1 Corinthians 14:34–36, in which the woman is "commanded" not to speak in church and 1 Timothy 2:11–15 in which the woman is "commanded" not to teach. We will deal later in our study with different interpretations of these passages, but, for the moment, it is sufficient to say that the New Testament itself will not allow for an interpretation of these passages as universals.

In the New Testament we find examples of women speaking in churches and teaching. We must understand those passages that prohibit these practices as particular to a certain time and place—or else we are forced to say that in the New Testament churches we have examples of women breaking God's universal laws.

4. Rules and goals for the Christian life understood in light of relationship to God.

In terms of our study of the Bible and women, it is important to notice that the rules and goals for the Christian life are exactly the same for men and women. The point is that, from what we see in the Bible, the woman is no second-class citizen for whom the ideals must be scaled down. She is as perfectly capable as the man in growing in Christlikeness.

5. Read the Bible in the light of Jesus.

So much could be said here, but I will limit myself to one passage: Luke 11:27–28. A woman calls out from the crowd that the mother of Jesus must have been one happy woman. Jesus responded that the truly happy woman is the woman who finds the will of God and does it. Jesus was not saying that marriage and motherhood cannot be a happy and meaningful experience for a woman, or that a woman does not have a responsibility to her husband and family if she is married. He was simply saying that a woman is more than a wife and mother. She is a child of God, created in God's image; she has a responsibility to find God's specific will for her life and do it. This responsibility is a more important one than any of the others she has. Jesus broke many barriers of his day in his dealings with the women with whom he came in contact, but he was probably the most radical in seeing the woman as more than a role imposed on her by the society of the day.

We turn our attention now from tools of biblical interpretation to the Bible itself. We will study the Old Testament, then the New, believing that careful study and openness can provide the keys we need to understand what the Bible has to teach about women.

Chapter 2

The Old Testament and Women

The Creation Narratives

The book of Genesis contains three creation narratives (1:1–2:3; 2:4–4:26; 5:1–2). Genesis 5:1–2 serves as the prologue to the genealogies that follow. For our purposes, we will concentrate on the first two narratives and try to answer the following questions:

(1) What are the differences between the two narratives?

(2) Is it possible that Genesis 2:4–4:26 was simply intended to be a more detailed account of Genesis 1:1–2:3?

(3) What were the concerns of the day for the writers of these narratives?

(4) How have these narratives been interpreted throughout Christian history?

(5) How did the New Testament writers understand and use these narratives?

(6) How did Jesus understand and use the narratives?

(7) How can we reconcile Genesis 1:1–2:3 and Genesis 2:4–4:26?

The striking difference between the first account of creation and the second is the creation of the woman. Genesis 1:26–29 speaks of one act of creation in which male and female were created in God's image. It seems that together they formed the image of God. They received the same commandments and were given the same responsibilities. In the second account the man was created first and the woman was created from the man and, in some sense, for him in that the other animals did not provide what he needed. The word for woman, we are told, is constructed on or from the Hebrew word for man.

Lest the interpretation begin to sound irredeemably chauvinistic, however, many scholars believe that the writer of the Genesis passage was speaking of equality in his or her use of the rib. The rib in that context, they say, implied equality and dignity. The writer certainly seemed to be saying that man is incomplete without woman. He or she may have been trying to say that the inequality between man and woman in his or her society was the result of sin. The author was exploring the entrance of sin into the world and the results of man and woman's willful disobedience.

Two other problems in this text have long troubled theologians and Bible scholars. If indeed the world of this writer was as completely oriented toward the male as we think it was, why did the serpent speak first to the woman? It seems more natural that the man would have been addressed first, especially if the idea of the passage is that the man is in some way superior to the woman because he was created first. The other problem is interpreting Genesis 2:24 in which the man was told to leave his father and mother when he married and to be joined to his wife. Are we to understand this literally? Would the man actually leave his family, his tribe perhaps, and join that of his new wife? What we see in the Old Testament is the opposite: the wife left her family and tribe, if need be, and joined that of her husband. Why would the writer of this passage call for the opposite of what was happening in the life of the people? With these issues, we have enough differences to move on to the next question.

Is it possible that Genesis 2:4–4:26 was simply intended to be a more detailed account of Genesis 1:1–2:3? For me, the answer is no; this was not the case. Some differences are not easy to reconcile, one of which is the order of the things created. In Genesis 1 the creation of man and woman is the culmination, the climax, of the work of creation. In Genesis 2 the order of creation is man, plants, animals, woman. The author of Genesis 2 had his or her own theological purposes for writing. He or she wanted to talk about the entrance of sin into the world and the disobedience of the man and woman with the resultant barrier between them and God. These are themes that the author of Genesis 1 did not discuss.

From our modern-day perspective, it is not always easy or even possible to know exactly what issues of the day the writer of a book or passage of the Bible was trying to address (our question 3), but it is important to try to understand the passage in its original context before bringing our present-day concerns to it. For instance, we can probably say without a doubt that the role and place of the woman in the churches at the end of the twentieth century was not one of the concerns of these writers. Yet, what they wrote will speak to us and help us give answer to our concerns. We take seriously the history and culture out of which the Bible grew, yet we believe the message of the Bible transcends one particular culture. This is part of what we mean when we say the Bible is inspired.

A Babylonian account of creation called "Enuma Elish" has been found. When we read this account and consider what we find in Genesis, especially Genesis 1, it seems quite likely that one of the purposes for the writing of Genesis 1 was to respond, from the perspective of faith in Yahweh, to this Babylonian account of creation. "Enuma Elish" also helps us see more clearly what was unique about the Hebrews' understanding of creation.

Some similarities exist between the Genesis creation story and "Enuma Elish." Both Genesis and "Enuma Elish" present the physical world as consisting of the physical earth, heavens, and an underworld. In both, water is the dominant element and the world emerged out of chaos. Here the similarities end.

The differences are striking. In "Enuma Elish" gods and goddesses were born out of the watery chaos. They married, produced young, partied, drank, and—most of all—warred with one another. They used magic, both to protect themselves and to destroy their enemies. We read of a terrible civil war between the gods. Some of the goddesses gave birth during this time to dragons and serpents to fight on their side. The victor of the war demanded total allegiance to himself as god of gods. He killed one of the lesser gods and drained his blood. From this blood the beings who lived on the earth were created.

It seems fair to say that in his or her day the author of Genesis 1 was calling people out of darkness into light. He or she was trying to answer the theological concerns of the day: to describe the true, one God and to describe this God's relationship with the beings of this earth—beings that God had created in God's image. God had not just created the male human beings in God's image but the female beings also. For that day, this was a remarkable statement. In fact, for our day, it is still a remarkable and marvelous statement.

Our next task is to see how these creation narratives in Genesis have been interpreted throughout Christian history (question 4). Most interpreters before this century accepted the male-oriented theory of Genesis 2. Adam has been considered, in some sense, superior because he was created first. This logic, of course, demands that the woman be thought of as inferior. The serpent spoke with Eve first because—as the inferior of the two—she would be weaker, more gullible, and easier to deceive. Pregnancy and childrearing became the woman's lot, made all the harder because she is part of a sinful world and is a sinner herself. Later, in secular fields, this came to be known as the "anatomy is destiny" theory, the idea that simply being born female relegated a woman to an inferior status in life.

In some of the feminist literature, especially in our day, we find attempts to explain away the "male is superior" theory that emerges from a particular understanding of Genesis 2, 3, and 4. If the order of creation is from the lowest form of life to the highest form of life, the argument goes, then the woman is actually presented in the Bible as being superior to the man, since she was created last. The serpent then spoke to Eve, not as the weaker of the two, but, rather, as the more intelligent. The serpent thought that by conquering the superior being first, the inferior would surely fall, too.

This reasoning is tempting, but we reject it. First of all, we are not allowed by the text to apply the lowest to highest form of life order found in Genesis 1 to Genesis 2 also. They are separate and different accounts with different agendas. The other, and more important, thing to say is that, taking the Bible as a whole, we cannot argue for the superiority of one human being over another, or of one sex over another. As women, we must be satisfied with equality.

I have often wondered about Genesis 2:24 (in which the man is told to leave his family upon marriage) in light of a paper written by an African graduate student at Southwestern Seminary in the 1970s. This young man compared the nomadic tribes of Africa, especially his own tribe, with what we see in the Old Testament. The main difference in the two tribal structures was that his African tribe was matriarchal. I have asked myself if Genesis 2:24 may be a remnant or a fragment of an earlier time in the history of the nation, a time when the structure of the society was matriarchal rather than patriarchal. If so, it could well be that the society was still using a phrase from its past without a lot of thought about the incongruities. In the same way, many young North American women use an old marriage vow—because it is beautiful and traditional—in which they promise to love and obey their husbands, when obeying their husbands is the last thing on earth they intend to do. The grooms of these young women promise as emptily to endow their wives with all their worldy goods. My point is that we can see how older, outmoded phrases are still used even after they cease to reflect reality.

If indeed the societal structure of the Genesis period was matriarchal, we may better understand why the serpent spoke first to Eve. In a matriarchal society that would have been the natural thing to do. We do not know and cannot know why the writer of this passage had the serpent speak first to Eve, nor what he or she was trying to say by having the story happen in this way, if anything. Maybe it was as simple as that Eve just happened to be closer to the serpent as the serpent approached. Maybe, as one short Old Testament professor suggested, Adam was too short to reach the fruit. More vital issues are at stake in this passage. We do a disservice to the author and to God who inspired the writing to get so entangled in the non-essentials that we miss the essentials.

It is important to our study to note how the writers of the New Testament used the Genesis passages (question 5). In 1 Corinthians, Paul wanted women to wear veils when they prayed and prophesied in church. We do not know why, and for our purposes it does not matter. In chapter 11, verse 7, however, Paul argues that the man should not cover his head because he is the image and glory of God, but that it is all right for the woman to cover her head because she is the glory of man. It seems from verse 8 that the woman is the glory of the man rather than God because man was created first and woman was made for man. Here we have all the elements of the "man is superior by virtue of having been created first" theory. It is important to remember that this theory can only be expounded by emphasizing Genesis 2 and ignoring Genesis 1, which is what Paul did. He did, however, do some back-tracking in verses 10–12, leaving him close to the "equality in the Lord" camp.

1 Timothy 2:13–14 is another good example of the "superior by virtue of having been created first" theory. A woman must be quiet, learn in submission, not be in authority over men, and not teach—because Adam was created first, then Eve. The writer even says that Adam was not deceived in the fall, a theological problem that we will take up later. The conclusion is verse 15, which is the biblical version of the "anatomy is destiny" theory: motherhood is the woman's lot in life.

The examples from 1 Corinthians and 1 Timothy are enough to show us that, in order to subdue the woman, a particular understanding of Genesis 2 is necessary. One must interpret the writer of Genesis 2 as intending to say that the woman is inferior because she was created second and from the man. One must also ignore completely Genesis 1 and the equality between man and woman that is clearly taught, and this is what 1 Corinthians 11:7 and 1 Timothy 2:13–14 have done. I stress this to highlight what I want to say about Jesus' understanding and use of the creation accounts (question 6).

Jesus was asked a question about divorce. His answer, appearing in its complete form in Mark 10:2–12 and Matthew 19:1–12, is a unique combination of Genesis 1:27—"So God created man in his own image, in the image of God he created him; male and female he created them"—and Genesis 2:24—"Therefore a man leaves his father and his mother and cleaves to his wife, and they become one flesh." Jesus chose to use the two passages most favorable to women. In one stroke he gave the woman equality in marriage, an equality she had never enjoyed. She is equal in marriage, said Jesus, because she is equal in creation. With this Jesus totally destroyed the norm of the day that gave the man the sole decision as to whether or not the marriage would continue, and deprived the woman of a voice in the matter. Equality implies both liberty and responsibility. This exegesis of Genesis 1 and 2 by Jesus can serve as our guide in many difficult interpretations if we will allow it to do so. In our task we will allow it to do so and will return to it again.

Genesis 2:4–4:26 (question seven) since they are, as we have seen, quite different. We reconcile them the only way we can by saying that they are both true. It is true that God created man and woman as equals, and they are, therefore, equals. It is also true that in a sinful world, it has proven so difficult as to seem impossible to live and relate as equals. Genesis 2 is, therefore, also true.

Old Testament Cultural Structures and their Effects on Women

We often assume that the structures of society found in the Bible must represent God's will; that is to say, God must have approved of them or they would not have been as they were. This assumption is often a mistake, because the structures of biblical societies were affected by sin just as ours are. We can, in fact, interpret the Old Testament to show that the ideal society from God's point of view would have been quite different from that which emerges from the Bible.

Three cultural structures of the Old Testament that negated women will be examined to explain this theory. We will see in what ways or how the structures devalued women, and we will ask whether or not the very existence of the structures represented the ideal will of God. The three structures are the monarchy, war, and the system we find in the Old Testament of priests and sacrifices —the priesthood.

As we read the Old Testament, we see that a woman was sometimes seen as primarily existing to provide a man, especially a king, with whatever he needed or wanted. King David needed a warm body to sleep with him and help keep him warm as he was dying. No medical reason exists that this warm body needed to be a beautiful young virgin, but lovely Abishag the Shunammite was chosen anyway (1 Kgs 1:1–4). In the opening passages of the book of Esther, King Ahasuerus needed to display his beautiful wife as yet another of his valuable treasures; and when she did not go along with the plan, he needed to make sure that she and all the other women of the province learned that this sort of independent thinking would not be tolerated (Esth 1). Solomon had a thousand wives, many of whom represented little more than a political or military alliance.

In all fairness it must be said that women were not the only segment of society to suffer under the monarchy. 1 Samuel 8:10–18 is a description of what life would be like under a human king, one who would use his people as little more than slaves and take for himself and his family the best of the produce of the land. The people of Israel could never say that they were not duly warned of the consequences of their decision to have a human king. They were not deterred from their head-strong decision to be like the other nations of the world, however, and God told Samuel to let them have their way (1 Sam 8:4–7). The monarchy was not God's idea nor preference but rather a concession to the people's stubborn will. The monarchy was a rejection of God who had offered to be and who had hoped to be the people's king.

War was another structure of ancient society that devalued women. Young virgins were often taken as part of the booty of war to become wives, concubines, or slaves for the conquering people. Non-virgins were often killed along with the men and children. We find an effort to provide a measure of protection to these captive wives in Deuteronomy 21:10–14. If the man decided he did not want the woman after he had brought her home and slept with her, he had to free her. She could not be sold as a slave. There was to be no monetary advantage to bringing these women home. This protection helped women some, but it did not change the fact that they were part of the loot, along with the cattle and sheep.

Women were also devalued by war because in the society their monetary value was roughly half that of a man. We read in Leviticus 27:1–9 of a special vow of persons to the Lord, and we see that at every age the male was valued more than the female. Perhaps there are other considerations, but we can see that, in a society dependent on war, men as warriors and boys as potential warriors would be valued more than women. This probably also helps explain why a woman would be considered unclean twice as long after the birth of a girl than after the birth of a boy. The society would be anx-ious to put the women who gave birth to boys back into circulation, in hope of producing more boys. We will look at the passage in more detail later.

There is no doubt that the Israelites fought many wars and that they often credited God with the victory, sometimes even the strategy. It is possible to accept the truth of this, while at the same time interpreting the Old Testament to say that war was never God's ideal. Indeed, war in the Old Testament is represented as a lack of faith in God's ability to provide without the necessity of violence. Baptist thinking on war in the Old Testament has, as a rule, been to accept that what we have are "holy wars" in which God fought on the side of God's people, at least to the extent that the particular war was "just." There is certainly a sense in which this seems to be the best interpretation of some of the battles. Even holy war, however, is a concession to the people's lack of faith.

God's ideal was that God would fight the people's battles for them. God would not fight with them but would rather fight instead of them. See Exodus 14:14, for example—"The Lord will fight for you, and you have only to be still"—or Deuteronomy 1:30—"The Lord your God who goes before you will himself fight for you, just as he did for you in Egypt before your eyes"—or Joshua 10:10–11, a battle in which God threw the enemy into a panic, then battered them with great stones from heaven. This is not to say that the Israelite army did not kill some of the enemy also, but "there were more who died because of the hailstones than the men of Israel killed with the sword" (Josh 10:11). The point of the writer seems to be that God was perfectly capable of handling things alone.

Had the people had the faith to accept it, God seemingly would have, using God's own devices, simply driven the inhabitants out of the promised land. Exodus 23:23–28 is a good passage to illustrate this. God promised to send an angel with the people as they went into the land. Verse 28 tells us that God would send hornets to drive out some of the people. Verse 27 talks of the terror that God would send—perhaps the hornets—that would throw all the people into confusion, and would "make all your enemies turn their back to you." In Judges 7, we read of a battle in which (v. 22) "the Lord set every man's sword against his fellow and against all the army." 1 Samuel 7 tells of a potential battle with the Philistines that never took place because (v. 10) "the Lord thundered with a mighty voice that day against the Philistines and threw them into confusion." Confusion of a similar kind is what takes place in 1 Samuel 14:1–23. In another passage, 2 Kings 7, the Lord had made (v. 6) "the army of the Syrians hear the sound of chariots, and of horses, the sound of a great army . . . so they (v. 7) fled away." David understood the truth of this when he said in 1 Samuel 17:45 that the Lord does not save with the sword and the bow; therefore, he, David, had come only with the name of the Lord.

Deuteronomy 6:10–19 speaks of God's promise to give the Israelites "great and goodly cities, which you did not build, and houses full of all good things, which you did not fill, and cisterns hewn out, which you did not hew, and vineyards and olive trees, which you did not plant." It hardly seems possible that this description of simply going in and moving into the houses of the cities would have been possible if the land had been taken by war. Part of the strategy of the battles seems to have been to destroy the crops and burn the cities. Again in Deuteronomy 11:22–25 we find God's promise to drive out the nations before Israel if the nation would only be careful to keep God's commandments. War became necessary because the people did not keep God's commandments.

It seems to me that what we have in the Old Testament concerning war is the following: God's ideal was that the people have sufficient faith to make it possible for them to enter the promised land without resorting to war. When that proved to be impossible, too risky, God proposed a strictly volunteer army that God would lead. Deuteronomy 20:1–9 shows us that men who had just built a new house, or planted a new vineyard, or gotten married did not have to fight. Neither did the men who were afraid. If a man did not want to fight, he did not have to. What was left was an army made up entirely of volunteers.

The volunteer army, apparently, proved to be too risky also; because by the time of the monarchy, there was a permanent, standing army that was supported by the taxes of the people. By this time, the faith of the people was almost entirely in their military strength rather than in God's ability to provide for them, so God bowed out of the situation. The Psalmist wrote, "Yet thou hast cast us off and abased us, and hast not gone out with our armies" (Ps 44:9). To believe in the power of the army rather than in the power of God was idolatrous; God could take no part in this.

The belief that war was never God's ideal also helps us understand one of the most difficult of all the commandments of the Bible: God's commandment to devote all the booty of war to God—that is, to kill the people and animals and destroy the things. The nation did not want to obey God's commandment and often did not, for which they faced the wrath of the prophets who insisted that it was clearly God's commandment. By giving this command, God was attempting to eliminate the motivation for fighting in the first place. If the nation could not enrich itself by war—and the nation clearly could not if it kept God's command—why risk lives?

The third cultural structure of the Old Testament that negated women was the priesthood. The system of priests and sacrifices devalued women in that it was open only to men in the Israelite nation. This seems strange, because the other nations of that time had women priests as well as men. Why would one nation exclude its women? Also, how do we explain that Miriam was certainly part of what seems to have been the first priestly team? We will discuss this and other questions and problems that relate to this Old Testament religious, cultural structure.

One of the main problems in trying to understand the priesthood and the sacrifical system is that we do not know for sure that God ordained this system from the beginning. We assume that God did. The usual interpretation is that God ordained the Old Testament sacrificial system but came to despise it because of the abuses and because the people finally put their faith in the system rather than in God. This may still be the best interpretation, but we cannot accept it without taking several factors into account.

Jeremiah wasn't certain that sacrifices had been the most important matter to God from the beginning of the nation. Jeremiah 7:22–23 reads: "For in the day that I brought them out of the land of Egypt, I did not speak to your fathers or command them concerning burnt offerings and sacrifices. But this command I gave them, 'Obey my voice, and I will be your God, and you shall be my people; and walk in all the way that I command you, that it may go well with you.' " This may have been a minority opinion, but it seems to have been the opinion of Jesus, too. Twice he said to the Saducees and Pharisees, "Go and learn the meaning of this: I desire mercy, not sacrifice." Other Old Testament voices tell us, too, that God wants a humble spirit, a contrite heart, or justice, instead of sacrifices.

The problem is that we cannot go back to a time when there were no sacrifices. The people offered sacrifices from the start of biblical references. Cain and Abel did; so did Noah. The Israelites offered sacrifices in Egypt, or would have if they could have. One of the reasons Moses gave Pharoah for letting the people go into the wilderness was to offer sacrifices to their God. The question is: Did God institute what we see or did God work with the people where they were, attempting to move them in another direction?

It seems possible that God allowed the system of sacrifices to exist and did what could be done to redeem it while trying to move the nation to a better way of relating to God. We see a tension between two ways of relating to God in the sacrifical system and the prophetic tradition. One could relate himself or herself to God through the priestly system of temple or altar, priest, and sacrifice or the person could go more directly to God; or perhaps it is better to say that God could deal more directly with the person through the prophetic traditon of prophet, experience, and Word of God. The prophetic tradition was more open, more dynamic, and apparently—from the beginning—included women as well as men. The Word of God was free to come to anyone; it could not be controlled.

It seems fair to say that we still see these two ways of relating to God in the New Testament in the tension between the Saducees and the Pharisees. The Saducees related to God through temple, priest, and sacrifice. The Pharisees were the lay preachers who emphasized the Word of God.

There was tension within the Old Testament community between those who thought that only the priests were holy to God and those who believed the nation as a whole was holy. "A kingdom of priests and a holy nation" is how Exodus 19:6 phrases it, and the Old Testament passage that Peter later used to speak of the church as "a chosen race, a royal priesthood, a holy nation, God's own people" (1 Pet 2:9). The movement during the exile toward synagogue rather than temple, and prayer and good deeds rather than sacrifice, surely moved the people closer to the "holy nation" concept and the importance of the laity. From the post-exilic book of Haggai, we see that the priests had a difficult time convincing the people that the temple must be rebuilt after the exile. The people were content to live in their nice houses while the temple remained in ruins. Surely one of the reasons for this vacillation is that the "holy people" theory had served them well during the exile.

Another problem in trying to understand the importance and meaning of the sacrificial system in the Old Testament is that we cannot be certain just what the sacrifices meant to the people. Undoubtedly the system in some sense made atonement for them, or they understood that it did. In some sense the animal bore the sin, so to speak, for the guilty human being.

There is another sense in which we can say that the sacrificial system was an economic issue. It was costly to give the best to God. A family could not eat the animal that was offered as sacrifice. While a family was expected to give the best that it could afford to God, the poor were not left out. They could bring birds, for instance, instead of sheep. What was not permitted, however, was to give to God the worst, the throwaway, instead of the best.

The prophets railed against the people for bringing the blind, the lame, and the sick animals thinking that these gifts were good enough to comply with the letter, if not the spirit, of the law. "Atonement is costly" was surely one of the messages God hoped to get across with the sacrificial system. This was surely David's understanding in the story we find in 2 Samuel 24. Araunah would have given David the threshing floor that David wanted. After all, David was the king, and it was for a good cause: to build an altar to God. But the king said to Araunah, "No, but I will buy it of you for a price; I will not offer burnt offerings to the Lord my God which cost me nothing."

Whatever else we say about the sacrificial system —whether we think God wanted it or not, what we think the sacrifices meant or did not mean—we must be clear about two facts. One is that, even if God did institute or ordain what we have in the Old Testament, it was intended to be temporary. God eventually intended that the people relate to God through faith in the one God would send, not through a system of animal sacrifices. Also, God was never obligated to or by the sacrificial system as the only way people could receive forgiveness or as the only thing that would make atonement for their sins. We must take seriously the half dozen or so examples we find in the Old Testament in which something other than a blood sacrifice made atonement for sin, for example: a live animal (Lev 16:9–10), money (Exod 30:11–16), incense (Num 16:46–47), Moses' prayer (Exod 32:30–32), an animal or flour (Lev 5:1–7; 11–13), the booty from war (Num 31:50), and—perhaps the most interesting example of all—a murder (Num 25).

We must be willing to say that God is God. Atonement or pardon comes from God, not from any system. If God chooses to accept something other than the usual blood sacrifice to make atonement, God is free to do so. What God accepts makes atonement.

We have touched on some of the major problems involved in trying to understand the Old Testament system of sacrifice. We still need to deal with two other topics. One is the question of why women were excluded from the priesthood in the Old Testament. The other is to ask if women should be excluded from the pastorate in our day because there were no Old Testament women priests.

One possible answer as to why women were excluded from the Israelite priesthood is that Israel was very concerned that people not think of God as a sexual being. Though the writers of the Old Testament often used the human analogy of father to speak of God, they did not mean to suggest that God is a male. We find a few examples in which God is depicted as a mother. The point is that God, who is neither male nor female, but Spirit, relates to us as loving parents relate to their human offspring. In the religions of Israel's neighbors, the gods were believed to be both males and females who actually had sexual intercourse and produced young. Many times the human priests and priestesses had sexual intercourse as part of the religious service. By excluding women, Israel gave the nation a one-of-a-kind priesthood, symbolic of and testimony to larger truths.

Another possible answer may be found in the Hebrew understanding of impurity and defilement by blood. Leviticus 15:19–31 shows us what daily life was like for the Hebrew women during times of bleeding, monthly periods, after childbirth, and hemorrhages. For at least seven days a month and for several weeks after childbirth, the woman was prohibited from even entering the temple. Needless to say, she could not have carried out the functions of the priest. This may help explain why she was excluded.

We are left with the confession that we do not know and cannot know why women were left out of the priesthood of their day. What we must be careful not to say or to imply is that God left them out because they were in some sense inferior to men. God seems ideally to have wanted a society in which there would be no priests, male or female. For this reason it seems weak to argue that women cannot be pastors in our day because there were no women priests in biblical times. God looked forward to moving the people to the understanding that God was the only priest they needed. It is hoped that in the church we have come to that place. We go to God directly through Jesus, our high priest. We hope that we will not exclude women again and use as our argument and model a system that in its own day was intended to be replaced with something better.

I have intended in this section to raise some questions about the cultural structures of monarchy, war, and priesthood that we have in the Old Testament, and to suggest that the structures of society we find in the

Bible do not represent God's ideal will. God did not
wish that women be considered as part of the booty of
war, nor that they be treated as little more than sex
objects by the various kings of the day. God did not
wish a religious structure that excluded women—the
priesthood—to exist forever. Had Israel had the faith,
God could have given the nation a different society. In
a society free of war, the people could have enjoyed the
peace that only God can bring. A peaceable kingdom
with God as king and God as priest and all God's
creatures living and working together as equals could
have been theirs. We do not fault them. We know in
our hearts that we, too, lack the faith. But how we wish
this society could be modeled for us!

The Reality of Life in the Old Testament

Sociologists tell us that the ancient Hebrew family
structure was similar to the family structure of the
other nations of that day. Families were extended; they
were made up of the partriarch, his wife or wives, any
unmarried daughters, the sons and their wives, grand-
children, and so on to include as many generations of
the family as might be living at any particular time. The
family also included the servants and their families and
the livestock.

Families were endogamous; they looked for spouses
for the children within the extended family. The ideal

marriage was thought to be between first cousins. They were patrilineal; they counted their lineage through the males. The appearance of the name of a woman in an Old Testament genealogy would have indicated that the author was making a specific point. Families were patrilocal; the burial place of the patriarch was considered to be the home territory of the tribe. Families were also patriarchal and polygynous. The patriarch made the final decision in cases of conflict; he could also have more than one legal wife.

Family structure shaped societal structure. The practical every-day realities of the family and societal structures of the day for the woman meant that she had no real place in the society except through her relationship to a man—her father, brother, son, or husband. The woman joined her husband's tribe upon her marriage, if she was not already a member of that tribe. The woman had no divorce rights and no voice in her husband's right to divorce her. The major decisions that affected all the society were made by men, the elders at the gate. The religious system of the day in the Hebrew culture excluded the participation of women, as we have noted.

The prejudice toward women and stereotyping of women that existed in the society can be seen clearly in some biblical passages. In Isaiah 19:16 someone trembled in fear as a woman. Jeremiah 31:22 speaks of something new: a woman protected a man. The passage in Judges 9:52–54 tells us of Abimelech's death in battle. The true death blow was dealt by a woman who threw an upper millstone from the top of a tower and crushed his skull. Abimelech asked his young armor-bearer to quickly draw his sword and kill him, lest it be said that a woman killed him.

The "tokens of virginity" passage in Deuteronomy 22:13–21 is difficult to understand. It is anyone's guess what these tokens would have been; bloody bedclothes is probably the best interpretation. We know, however, that not every woman bleeds the first time she has sexual relations, and that it is quite possible that some innocent women died. The punishment was severe enough for the man who falsely accused his wife, however, that it would have been foolhardy to accuse her if the tokens existed. In this passage we can clearly see the male orientation of the society and the prejudice that existed toward the woman and how she sometimes, perhaps often, suffered because of it. We see something else at work, however, in the punishment meted out to the man who falsely accused his wife. We see a kind of counter reality at work in the society; we see God doing everything possible to provide for women protection and dignity within the societal structure.

The Counter Reality

We have said that the Old Testament society was a male-oriented one. Men had the power, the vote. Men were the priests and the kings. We have also said that the society in the Old Testament did not represent God's ideal will. Why didn't God simply put into being the ideal society? It was not possible. God is limited by human sin; God cannot reveal more of God's will to us than we are willing to receive; God cannot lead us any further down God's path than we are willing to be led. God did do what was possible, working within and through the reality that existed, to provide women rights and protection.

Some persons of that day caught the vision of equality for all human beings under God and passed it on to us. When God came in Jesus Christ, that reality was brought into perfect focus, because Jesus lived it out in every human contact of his earthly life. We grasp the vision of this reality, and it is all we need. We can confidently read the Old Testament believing that, in God's eyes, men and women are equals, and that God was doing everything possible in the laws given and in the things revealed to the nation to help the people grasp this truth. What follows is my attempt to read the Old Testament in light of the question: What is God trying to do for women in these passages?

It is immediately clear in the Old Testament that women had rights under the law, not only married women with a secure place within the family, but women at all levels of society. We mentioned earlier the rights or protection that the law gave the foreign women who were brought back as part of the booty of war (Deut 21:10–14). These women were not to be treated as slaves. The law protected women slaves, also. Exodus 21:7–11 shows us that a man could not sell his female slave; he could not mistreat her if he or his son (if she married his son) was displeased with her. This passage also shows us the circumstances under which she was allowed to be redeemed. The law protected the seduced virgin (Exod 22:16). The man who seduced a virgin either had to marry her or pay the marriage price.

The vision that God was the woman's friend in the Old Testament provides us with clues to help interpret other difficult passages. According to Leviticus 12:1–7, the woman was considered to be unclean twice as long after the birth of a female child as after the birth of a male. From our perspective, there seems to be no explanation other than the one that the society preferred boy babies to girl babies and wanted to put the woman bearing boys back into circulation quickly.

We must not become so entangled, however, in trying to give an answer as to why there were two different time periods that we miss the point of the law in the first place. A woman needs time after childbirth to recuperate physically and emotionally. To have sexual relations too soon can be physically damaging. When we consider that the length of time modern medicine says is essential for recuperation is exactly the length of time given in this passage, we can fairly say that this passage is God's prenatal course for the men of that day.

Our assumption that God is on the side of women also helps us shed some positive light on Numbers 5:11–31. This passage deals with the test of jealousy; the jealous husband had the right to put his wife through a humiliating and physically painful trial if he suspected her of adultery. Israel was not unique in this practice. The Hammurabi Code, for instance, required the accused wife to cast herself into the sacred river. It was believed that the guilty ones drowned; the innocent wives would manage to survive.[1]

In Israel, the jealous husband did not have the right to judge the accused wife. God was the judge. This is not to diminish the fact that the practice itself was unjust, especially that there was no punishment for the husband who accused his wife unjustly, but God did not institute the practice itself. God did, however, make it clear how the practice would be carried out. Justice was not left in the hands of the jealous husband, but rather in those of a merciful God. In this we see the hand of God.

The Hebrew woman also had the right to make and to carry out a vow to God. Numbers 30 deals with the right of the father or husband to repudiate a vow made by a daughter or wife. In some sense, this offered the women a measure of protection, especially in the case of a vow she made hastily or unwisely. It is difficult to explain away the patronizing tone of the passage, however. The fact that women did make vows to God must not be missed; we have some examples of this in the Old Testament. For instance, Numbers 6:2 and following shows us that men or women were permitted to take the stringent Nazirite vow. The vow Hannah made in 1 Samuel 1:11 to give her son to the Lord is made all the more forceful and touching by the knowledge that her husband had the right to repudiate her vow.

Although, as a rule, the property and goods of a family were passed down from father to son—that is to say, male to male—a woman did have the right to inherit in some cases. Caleb's daughter (Josh 15:19) and the daughters of Zelophehad (Josh 17:3–6) received an inheritance. The daughters of Job, along with their brothers, inherited (Job 42:15). (The latter example is interesting in that the daughters of Job are named, and their brothers are not.)

It appears that women had the right to work at jobs that were traditionally held by men. We read in 1 Chronicles 7:24 of a woman who built cities. In Nehemiah 3:12 we see that women helped rebuild the walls of the city. We know from the background that they, like the men, did this at the risk of life. The judges of Israel were usually men, but at one point in the history of the nation, the prophetess, Deborah, was chosen (Judg 4, 5). She earned a mighty reputation for all time as a woman greatly used of God. Like the election of a prophet, the election of the judges was not in the hands of the people. The Spirit came to whomever God wished. All that seems to have been required was an openness to God.

It is generally thought that the people of Old Testament times believed that the inability to have children was the fault solely of the woman. At least one author of the Old Testament materials took a step beyond. Deuteronomy 7:14 reads, "You shall be blessed above all peoples; there shall not be male or female barren among you, or among your cattle." The barren women deserved to be given the consideration of the doubt.

The overall picture of the Old Testament is one of a great deal of freedom for women within the confines of the society. The writers of certain New Testament books were actually more concerned that women be submissive than were the writers of the Old. Passages like 1 Peter 3:1–6 influence the way we read the Old Testament. Peter called upon the women in his day to be submissive to their husbands as the holy women of old were submissive to theirs. He mentioned Sarah by name, pointing out that she obeyed Abraham, calling him Lord. When we go to the Old Testament, however, it is hard to decide which incidents in particular Peter had in mind. Old Testament women were certainly not submissive by the definition of submissive in our day. Usually by submissive we mean weak, passive, child-like. Sarah and her Old Testament sisters in the faith were verbal, even assertive at times, not in the least shy or timid about expressing their feelings or desires.

Sarah certainly wasn't submissive when she insisted that Hagar and Ishmael be put out to fend for them-selves. Rebekah was free to go to Canaan and marry Isaac or stay with her own people. After she married Isaac and bore his children, she ruined any possibility that her sons could relate to one another positively by her continual preferential treatment of Jacob. Rachel was not submissive in that she stole her father's idols and later went to great lengths not to be discovered. Rachel and Leah's relationship with one another and with Jacob is enlightening. In Genesis 30:14 and fol-lowing we find the story of Reuben bringing his mother Leah some mandrakes that Rachel wanted. So Rachel traded her right to sleep with Jacob that night for the mandrakes, and Leah went out to inform Jacob to which tent he should report when the sun went down. If there is a passive individual in this story, it is Jacob.

These were not passive, weak women. They enjoyed a great deal of freedom and had the liberty to make known their thoughts and wishes. We think of the Song of Solomon, for instance, in which the woman, as well as the man, is depicted as capable of and desirous of a strong, passionate, sexual love. Throughout much of the history that has flowed from the time of that writing, much of the world, including the church, has been uncomfortable with the idea that women are sexual beings in every sense of the word. The truth of the matter is that these women in the Old Testament enjoyed more freedom and were taken more seriously than many of the women we meet later in the Bible and throughout history.

It does not seem too farfetched to suggest that God included women, including these women, in God's plans for the world from the beginning. God appeared to Abraham at least three times. It is true that the appearances in chapters 12 and 15 of Genesis involve only Abraham, but Genesis 17 is another story. Sarah was as involved in the experience as Abraham. Her name would be changed also. He would become the father of nations, and she the mother of nations. I have heard many sermons on Abraham as the father of nations, but none that spoke of Sarah as the mother of nations. In the same way, I have heard sermons on the confession of Peter in Matthew 16. I have never heard a sermon on the confession of Martha in John 11 even though it was the same confession: "I believe that you are the Christ, the Son of God" (v. 27).

The Old Testament recognizes the tremendous influence of the wife and mother in the family and in the society. This is why we find some of the harshest words of the Old Testament directed to married women and mothers who were adulterers. It is interesting that the Old Testament takes a much softer stand toward the unmarried prostitute. She had no real place in the society and was forced to survive any way she could. The married woman, however, was part of the covenant. She was one of God's chosen people. With her adultery, she willfully chose to disregard her rightful and lawful place in society and to use her influence within her family and the society for bad rather than for good.

Influence is power. This is the truth the Bible speaks. Mothers and fathers are instructed in the Bible to use their influence over their children to bring the children up in the way of the Lord. The book of Ruth is a good case study of the "influence is power" theme. Ruth was a Moabitess. The origin of the Moabites was the incestous relationship between Lot and his virgin daughters (Gen 19:30–38). The Israelites despised the Moabites, mainly because the Moabites had not allowed them to cross through their territory as the Israelites were coming out of Egypt and had hired Balaam to curse them. We see in Deuteronomy 23:3–4 that Moabites were prohibited from ever entering the temple, meaning they could never really be a part of the

society. Yet, Ruth, a Moabitess, was the grandmother of
Israel's great King David and even had a place in the
genealogy of Jesus. How did it happen? We find the
answer in the words of Boaz in Ruth 2:10–11. "All that
you have done for your mother-in-law since the death
of your husband has been fully told to me."

The Old, "New" Vision: Proverbs 31

No study of the Old Testament is complete without
considering the picture of the woman we find in
Proverbs 31:10–31. In 1983 Grace Baruch, Rosalind
Barnett, and Caryl Rivers published their research
based on hundreds of interviews with women.[2] The
authors inquired about every aspect of their subjects'
lives, "trying to answer one central question—what
contributes to a woman's sense of well-being?" What
emerged the authors called, "a new vision of women's
lives." The basic thesis is that women need just what
men need: They need love and work. By love the
authors meant love of parents, siblings, friends, and
perhaps love of husband and children. By work the
authors meant competence in a field.

Their work showed that the happiest women are
those who are happily married, have a good relationship with their children, and have a job that they enjoy
and that provides them with a sense of competence.

The surprising result of their survey was that, while marriage and family can greatly enrich life for women, husband and children do not fill all of a woman's needs. Most societies teach women to look to marriage and family to fill every need; but the truth of the matter is that the unhappily married woman with an unhealthy relationship with her children, and perhaps no work or work that does not fill her needs, is much more unhappy than the single woman who has a job she enjoys and the love of family and friends. The survey also shows that it is good for the husband and children if the wife and mother works at a job she enjoys and experiences the satisfaction of work.

Lifeprints is an excellent and timely book, but the "new vision" is not new. It is rather the description of the ideal woman as portrayed by the writer of Proverbs thousands of years ago. The woman in Proverbs was a wife and mother. She was also a business woman. The conclusion we draw from the passage is that it is good for a woman's husband and children and herself for her to have interests outside the home. The woman in Proverbs obviously had money to call her own. (Discretionary money is power in any society.) She worked hard, but she and her family reaped the benefits of her hard work.

We know the thesis of *Lifeprints* is true. We see it is also a biblical truth. There is, however, a problem. The Bible does not tell us who cared for this woman's children while she took care of her business. Can we assume that the extended family filled her need for babysitters? Perhaps her husband helped? Women today have the same problem. We know we need to work, but it takes time to study and prepare for a career, and it takes time to work. A person can be only one place at a time and devote herself to only one thing at a time.

Lifeprints' answer is daycare, but it is not the answer for many women. Studies show that children brought up in daycare are sick more often than children reared at home. The caretakers of young children are poorly paid so there is high turnover in that field. It is difficult for babies and very young children to adjust constantly to new caretakers. Many mothers are not willing to have "latchkey" children if their jobs are not absolute necessities for the family's survival.

More participation from the husband and father is part of the solution. In many families, the wife's work is as important to the husband as is his own, and together they do the juggling necessary to have two careers and some semblance of family life. The woman needs more than this, however. She needs the society she lives in to take her and her needs seriously. She and her husband need liberal maternity and paternity leaves when new children come into the family. She and her husband need flexible work hours so that one of them can be with the children before and after school. Families need for the caregiving to young children to be a respected and well-paid profession so that daycare is truly an option for parents and a positive experience for children. Women and men must be willing to use their political muscles to say to those in power that we want our families and quality of life for all people to matter most.

For the Christian woman, who does not work outside the home, for whatever reason, the Christian life understood as vocation can fill her need for work or competence in a field. I am suggesting serious study of the Bible, of other religions, of the history of the Christian faith. I am talking about teaching, writing perhaps, counseling, talking with people about their relationship with God, speaking, even preaching, and working with groups seeking to bring about changes in church and society for the good of all. I am speaking of "pastoring," perhaps without ordination or salary. "That's not fair;" many will say, "she should be paid for what she does, just as the pastor is paid." They, of course, are right.

Realistically, however, the majority of women today will not be paid pastors. Some women can work for God's "well-done" while working toward and waiting for the changes that will take place in the church. In some churches the most respected person in the church is a woman, often an older woman, who has a profound knowledge of the Bible—that has come from

years and years of reading and studying it—and whose
life is a shining example of what God can do with any
of us if we will open our hearts and minds and very
lives to God. In fact, when salaries and ordination do
come, with the accompanying expectations and pres-
sures, we will realize that there is a lot to be said for
the consecrated life of the laity.

Notes

[1]Louis M. Epstein, *Sex Laws and Customs in Judaism* (New
York: KTAV Publishing, 1968) 217-18.

[2]Rosalind Barnett, Grace Baruch, and Caryl Rivers,
Lifeprints: New Patterns of Love and Work for Today's Women
(1983).

Chapter 3

The Gospels

While the cultural structures of the world of the Old Testament were definitely chauvinistic, life was not as bleak for the women as we are sometimes led to believe. God was woman's friend. Many people of that day understood this truth. The people of the New Testament world had to learn it again. This truth was modeled for us in the way Jesus treated the women with whom he came in contact. The Gospel writers faithfully recorded these encounters. We turn our attention now to the four Gospels and what they teach about Jesus' attitude—God's attitude—toward women.

After studying the following Gospel passages, a student wrote: "We look in vain for one negative thing in the life of Jesus as far as women are concerned." He is right. When reading the Old Testament, we sometimes have to read with the conviction that God is woman's friend, looking for the positive. Not so with the Gospels. One would have to read into the text anything negative in Jesus' attitude toward women.

The Genealogy of Jesus (Matt 1:1–17)

Scholars have long been intrigued by the inclusion of women in the genealogy of Jesus. As a rule, Jewish genealogies, included only men. Making matters even more curious are the particular women that Matthew included. The first woman named is Tamar. We read about her in Genesis 38. She was the wife of Judah's eldest son, Er, who—according to the story—was wicked in the sight of the Lord and was, therefore, slain by the Lord. Since no children had been born to Tamar and Er, the second son was called upon to "raise up offspring for your brother." When Onan refused to do that, the Lord slew him also. At this point, Judah suggested to Tamar that she return to her father's house as a widow and wait until the third son was old enough to do the duty of the first born. When Judah reneged on that promise, Tamar disguised herself as a harlot and allowed herself to become pregnant by Judah himself. Though the Bible never condones harlotry, the story ends with the statement by Judah that she was more righteous than he, in that he did not keep his promise to her.

Rahab was another harlot, at least according to the translation of the majority of the versions of the Bible in English. The New International Version translates the Hebrew word, innkeeper, however. It does seem to be a bit odd that a harlot would be living with her parents and family. At any rate, she was a foreigner, and possibly a woman with a bad reputation. She distinguished herself, however, and saved herself and her family by helping the Hebrew spies when they scouted the city of

Jericho. Rahab married Salmon; they were the parents of Boaz, who married Ruth.

Ruth was a Moabitess. The Jews despised the Moabites as enemies and believed that they had originated in the incestous relationship between Lot and his daughters, and forbidden by law ever to enter the temple. Yet, Ruth found her honored place in Israelite society as the great-grandmother of King David.

Another woman included in the genealogy of Jesus was Bathsheba, wife of Uriah. She is remembered as having become pregnant by King David while her husband was away in battle and who later bore David's son Solomon.

While making no attempt to guess what the writer of the genealogy of Matthew intended to say by the inclusion of these women in the genealogy of Jesus, the least we can say is that the plans and purposes of God were broader than the prejudices of the Hebrew nation. By the time of Jesus sinners were harshly condemned. One message of the genealogy is that sinners can be redeemed and used by God. By the time of Jesus, there was within Jewish religious circles a firmly-fixed separation between Jews and non-Jews. One message of the genealogy is that God always has included and will surely continue to include all peoples in God's plans and purposes for the world. God includes those whom we reject. By the time of Jesus there were unscalable barriers between men and women in Jewish society.

Surely one message of the genealogy is to point out that throughout the life of the nation, God has included and worked God's will through women as well as men—not just good, moral, pure, Jewish women but all kinds of women. No one is beyond the reach of God's grace.

Jesus' Teaching on Adultery (Matt 5:27–30)

In Judaism, adultery was often seen as committed against a married man only. The woman who committed adultery committed it against her husband. The man who committed adultery committed it against the husband of the woman with whom he committed adultery. Therefore, adultery between a married man and a single woman or a married man and a non-Jew would not have been seen as sin, since there was no married Jewish man to whom to give offense. Jesus did not see it that way. Adultery was committed against the woman also, whatever her marital status or nationality. In fact, adultery was so grave an offense that Jesus dealt with the feelings and attitudes that led to adultery. The overt act was simply a continuation of sinful thoughts and desires. The man or woman who lusted in his or her heart had already treated another person as a sexual object and damaged his or her own relationship with God. Whatever the price of bringing lustful thoughts under control; it was worth it, Jesus said. Regarding adultery, Jesus elevated the status of woman, giving her equality with the man. Adultery was committed against both man and woman. Along with equality always comes responsibility. Woman is not a victim; she too is responsible for keeping her lustful thoughts and nature under control.

Jesus' Teaching on Marriage and Divorce (Matt 5:31–32; 19:1–9; Luke 16:18; Mark 10:2–12)

As we have said before, in the Jewish world the man had the exclusive right to divorce his wife. Even in the cases in which the wife appealed through the courts for a divorce, the husband was the one who actually had to divorce her. She never divorced him. Jesus said that the man who simply fulfilled the letter of the law by giving his wife a certificate of divorce was not justified but guilty. He had victimized an innocent person for she was forced to live with the stigma of divorce; and, if she remarried, she and her new husband shared the stigma. Jesus also said that when the divorcing husband remarried, he shared the stigma also. The point seems to be, in cases of divorce, that everyone who is involved pays.

Jesus called his hearers back to God's original ideal for marriage: one man and one woman in a relationship of mutual faithfulness that is ended only upon the death of one of them. Because the woman is created in the image of God, as is the man, she is an equal in the marriage relationship. As an equal, she deserves equal rights and equal say. This was never true in a sinful world. The divorce certificate became reality in the first place because human beings were sinners. As the original divorce certificate had provided the woman a measure of protection, the words of Jesus gave women further protection and dignity. Though divorce may have continued much as it had been practiced before Jesus spoke, the Jewish male could never again feel that he pleased God by simply keeping the letter of the law.

Renouncing Marriage for the Sake of the Kingdom (Matt 19:3–12)

It seems that Jesus' words about marriage made some of the disciples nervous. If God's intention was that a man stay with his wife for better or worse, maybe it was better for a man not to marry than to get into a relationship from which he could not simply be released. Jesus saw not marrying as a possibility if the option was celibacy. One does not reject marriage, however, out of fear of involvement or out of the idea that marriage is inferior to celibacy. They are both good options. The person chooses the one that seems best suited to him or her.

Marriage, a Temporal State (Luke 20:34–36)

Marriage is a "this-world" relationship. The procreation of the race is necessary for this time, and marriage and family are God's ordained way of continuing the race. This need will not continue into eternity. Men and women will not be known as husbands or wives or even as fathers and mothers. All will be called God's children. All distinctions of family, race, and nationality will disappear. There will be simply God's family, a family of equals. Perhaps because Jesus viewed life from this final perspective, he was able to rise above the society of the day in his view of the worth and ability of women.

Jesus' Teaching on the Will of God (Matt 12:46–50; Mark 3:31–35; Luke 8:19–21; 11:27–38)

For Jesus, finding the will of God and doing it received top priority. This took precedence over any of life's other activities, responsibilites, or relationships.

In a study session of the Gospel passages, one student wrote: "The only distinction Jesus made between people was between those who were doing the will of God and those who weren't." She is right. It is in the seeking and doing of the will of God that people put themselves in one camp or the other. This division cuts across all human differences be they sex, race, ethnic groups, rich, poor, young, old, well, ill. Those who do God's will are Jesus' family, bound to him and to each other in ways that no human family can be. Though Jesus never rejected his earthly family, and in his final hours assured that his mother would be cared for, he made it clear that his first alliegance was to God. In fact, Jesus insisted that finding God's will and doing it cannot be left until all of life's other obligations have been taken care of. God must come first.

As we have noted earlier, in Luke 11:27–28, Jesus said that even women have the responsibility to put God first. Even wives and mothers have this responsibility. This in no way indicates that women should neglect their families; neither should women use their families as an excuse not to do God's will.

Jesus Breaks Down the Barriers

Touching and Being Touched
(Matt 9:18–26 and parallels; 26:6–13 and parallels; Luke 7:11–15; 13:10–17)

So great was the fear of defilement on the part of the religious community during Jesus' day, that many restrictions existed concerning what could safely be touched. One would never touch the dirty, sick, or dead. In fact, everyday contact with the common people was thought to be defiling. Jesus called attention to himself in that he was willing to be with common everyday people. He ate in their homes. He called some of them to be his disciples. He touched them and allowed them to touch him.

The woman with the hemorrhage of blood lived a life of daily grind trying to keep the law of purification. (See Lev 15:19–27). Perhaps she had given up long before. She had faith that Jesus' touch would cure her, but she knew better than to ask a holy man to touch her. He was forbidden by the law to do so. With Jesus, she learned she was in the presence of a different kind of holy man. Jesus laid his hand on the woman who had been bent over for eighteen years and she straightened up. So great was his concern for the widow of Nain that he did the unthinkable: He touched the dead and gave back to this woman her only son. Jesus was willing to be touched. The anointing of Jesus with expensive perfume by the woman is a beautiful story of human devotion. Many scholars believe that this woman had been healed or forgiven by Jesus prior to this encounter—that is to say, she was not unknown to him. She, more clearly than the disciples at this point, grasped the fact that his ministry would cost Jesus his life. It seems she brought the most expensive and precious thing she owned, and Jesus allowed her to minister to him, to "waste" her resources in this way.

Interacting
(Matt 15:21–28 and parallels;
Luke 10:38–42; John 4:1–26; 8:1–11; 11:1–44)

In a world in which the pious never spoke to women in public, the ease with which Jesus engaged in conversations with women astonished many. The writer of the Gospel of John made it very clear that the conversation between Jesus and the Samaritan woman was not something that took place every day. Not only had Jesus engaged a woman in conversation, but a Samaritan woman, and not only a Samaritan woman, but a Samaritan woman of ill repute. She was understandably wary at first but, during the course of the encounter, moved from seeing Jesus as a Jew to the Savior of the world. Her contagious enthusiasm over the view of God that Jesus had presented to her and the possibility of a personal relationship with the Christ himself spilled over into her village, and the village people invited Jesus and the disciples to stay with them a while, which they did.

It seems fair to say that Jesus himself began a ministry among the Samaritans that continued to bear fruit. We read in Acts 8 that the Samaritans had already received the word of God when the disciples went to pray for them that they might receive the Spirit. The disciples did not seem to need the validation of speaking of tongues to assure them that this barrier to the gospel had been crossed as they did when the Gentiles and the disciples of John were converted.

Throughout the history of the church and synagogue, there has been much debate over the right of women to study and to receive the same theological education as men. As a rule, the woman has either been denied the privilege of a theological education, or she has been limited to certain areas of study such as education or music, but not theology. In some cases women were not allowed to take certain courses within a theological curriculum—for example, biblical languages or systematic theology. In the beautiful story at the end of Luke 10, Mary joined the group at Jesus' feet, the theological group. Interestingly enough, it was not the men but the other woman in the story who said that Mary did not belong there. On the contrary, Jesus said that she had chosen the "good portion." Theological study is good and helpful to men and women. The church needs the theological input of all its members.

Martha may have wanted Mary in the kitchen instead of at Jesus' feet the day Jesus came to lunch, but obviously she herself picked up some theology through her contact with Jesus. When her brother Lazarus became ill, Martha sent for Jesus to heal him. She was surely aware that Jesus had healed total strangers and probably expected him to come as quickly as he could to help his beloved friend. As difficult as it must have been for Martha to understand why Jesus had not come, her confidence in him was intact. Her confession is similar to the confession of Peter in Matthew 16, indicating that women, as well as men, had the capacity to recognize the Christ when he entered their lives.

The encounter between Jesus and the woman caught in adultery was not one that Jesus initiated. She was brought to Jesus. There was no doubt of her guilt. The law required that the adulterer or adulteress be caught in the very act of adultery, and that there be two witnessess. Under the law, she deserved to be put to death. We see the difference in Jesus and those who brought the woman to Jesus. They saw the woman through the eyes of their society: a guilty adulteress deserving death. Jesus saw the same person through the eyes of God: a person of great worth, loved by God, capable of being redeemed, and capable of living a different kind of life under God's love and guidance.

The encounter between Jesus and the Canaanite or Syrophoenician woman was of the woman's making. It is not clear why he ignored her at first, nor why he used the harsh, possibly derogatory phrase, "dogs." This woman, however, was not to be put off. She needed help desperately, and she knew Jesus could help her. She rose to the occasion in her response to him. Jesus recognized genuine faith when he saw it; the woman's daughter was healed, and the disciples got a crash course in God's broad acceptance of all peoples.

Including
(Matt 27:55–56; Mark 15:40–41; Luke 8:1–3; 23:49)

These verses speak volumes in our study of women. We see that, from the beginning, Jesus' disciples included women. They obviously traveled with Jesus and were present as he taught, healed, and proclaimed God's kingdom. We see that all levels of society were represented in this gathering of women. They helped support the ministry financially, and Jesus' ego was not damaged by that.

We now turn our attention to the cross and resurrection and see that these women were faithful beyond the final hour.

The Resurrection
(Matt 28:1–10; Mark 16:1–8;
Luke 24:1–11; John 20:1–18; 1 Cor 15:1–7)

Evelyn and Frank Stagg have an intriguing chapter on the resurrection in their book, *Woman in the World of Jesus*. According to the Staggs, the New Testament contains two traditions of the resurrection. One is the "empty tomb tradition" that gives priority to the women present at the tomb on the morning of the resurrection. The other is the "appearances tradition" that is found in 1 Corinthians 15:1–7 and that emphasizes the appearances of Jesus to the male disciples.[1]

Paul probably wrote the book of 1 Corinthians around AD 53. He said that the "appearances tradition" was the one he received and was passing on to them. The Staggs ask if it is probable that Paul was acquainted with the "empty tomb tradition" at the point of writing 1 Corinthians, but chose to use the other tradition. They answer, yes, it is probable that he knew of the tradition of the empty tomb but ignored it.

Why would Paul have ignored it? Because he and the other leaders of the church feared that the gospel would be jeopardized by a dependency on the testimony of women for its validity. Just as in courts of Jewish law the testimony of a woman was either not received or carried less force than that of a man.

Yet, when the Gospels were written later, all four recorded the appearance of the women at the tomb. This seems strange, considering that the church at this point had an "official" account of the resurrection (i.e., 1 Cor. 15:1–7) that served it well. Why stir up trouble? To make matters even more complicated, the accounts we find in the Gospels are impossible to reconcile. Differences exist in the time of the visit to the tomb, in the purpose of the visit, in the number and identity of women, the message received, the type of messenger, the reaction of the woman, the words of Jesus, and others. All that can be said with certainty is that some women were present at the tomb of Jesus on the

morning of the resurrection and received the commission to tell the others that he had risen from the dead.

Why would the gospel writers include an incident
that carried in it the seeds of future trouble? Only one
answer will suffice: They could not faithfully represent
the life of Jesus and leave out the presence of the
women at the tomb. Women were there; they received
their commission. This is the truth with which the
church must deal.

Jesus and the Twelve

Jesus did exclude women in that he did not choose a
woman to be one of the twelve. Some say that because
of this, women are necessarily excluded from the pastorate today. Others counter by arguing that following
such reasoning, only first-century Jewish males could
be eligible to be pastors of Christian churches today.
Both the argument and the counterargument miss the
point of why Jesus elected the twelve in the first place.

The best interpretation of the twelve is that Jesus
intended them to be a symbol: Twelve patriarchs were
in the old Israel and twelve in the new Israel. With this
symbol, Jesus demonstrated his intention to form a new
nation, a new people—to start again. In Acts 26:6–7,
Paul said in his defense before Agrippa that he was on
trial "for hope in the promise made by God to our
fathers, to which our twelve tribes hope to attain." With

the symbol of the twelve disciples, Jesus was saying to the tribes of Israel, "I am the promise of God made to your fathers."

We have noted some of the barriers of his day that Jesus broke. He spoke freely with women in public. He had women as intimate friends. Women disciples apparently followed him from the earliest days of his ministry and supported his ministry financially. In fact, none of the restrictions against women that one finds in the New Testament is attributed to him. Jesus opened the door of ministry to women. Why did the early church close it?

Notes

[1]Evelyn and Frank Stagg, *Woman in the World of Jesus* (Philadelphia: Westminster Press, 1978) chap. 6.

Chapter 4

The Early Church and Women

What we see in the New Testament concerning the acceptance, place, and role of women in the churches makes no sense apart from some understanding of the background in which the books were written. Without making an effort to understand what was going on in the wider world, it seems we have a mass of contradictions. Women were instructed not to teach; yet they taught. Women were told not to speak in church; yet they prayed and prophesied aloud in the church meetings. What was going on?

The Background

Although it took awhile, most of the leaders of the New Testament church finally came, through the help of the Spirit, to a great truth: God makes no distinction between persons. God favors no person over another. God rejects no one who comes to God. Knowing this and believing it are one thing; living out the practical implications is another, as the early church leaders knew.

The ideal church is one in which earthly differences between people do not exist: "There is neither Jew nor Greek, there is neither slave nor free, there is neither male nor female; for you are all one in Christ Jesus"

(Gal 3:28). During the time of the New Testament, this would have meant that Jews and Gentiles had to put aside ancient grudges in their effort to follow their Lord. It would have meant that masters and slaves changed status. They were no longer masters and mistresses and slaves but brothers and sisters in Christ, both parties free in Christ while indebted to him. In a society where slaves were regarded as little more than animals, this concept would have required a major shift in thinking and behavior. In the eyes of the society of the day, men and women were not considered equals. In the church, under the Lordship of Christ, they were. Ideally—within the New Testament church—man, woman, master, slave, Jew, or Gentile meant nothing. All people within the church were to be distinguished by their allegiance to Jesus Christ only.

Actually though, the distinctions remained. The rich ate with the rich at the fellowship meals, and the poor went hungry. The distinction between master and slave remained. The woman was asked to relinquish some of her new-found freedom and to submit herself to the authority of her husband.

The ideal church is one in which every child of God uses his or her God-given gifts for the good of the church. God, as sovereign Lord, is free to endow any person with any gift. The person has only to discover his or her gifts and follow through with the responsibility to use them in God's work. Unfortunately, human beings tend to rank gifts. This gift, we say, is more important than that one. Christians often become egotistical about the gifts they possess and use those gifts to bring attention to themselves instead of to God. We know we are guilty of this in our churches today. We only have to read the New Testament to know that the early Christians were guilty of this, also.

While the New Testament Christians had a hard time living out the ideals within the church, they lived them well enough to make the world around them nervous. The larger world did not understand or approve of giving slaves and women so much freedom. Many Jews did not understand how Gentiles could claim to have been accepted by God when they had not been circumcised and did not keep the law. The Romans feared a segment of society that felt no allegiance to the old gods.

The church of the New Testament had problems within and without. Without, the early church had to deal with persecutions, first by Jews, later by Romans. Early Christians had to cope with various misunderstandings. Because they rejected the gods of the day, they were accused of atheism. Because of confusion about their rituals, they were accused of cannibalism. Because they were mistrusted, hated, and feared, they were even accused of setting fire to Rome.

Within, the early church people struggled to work out their theology in the face of various false teachings and heresies. There were power struggles within the young church and personality clashes. Many persons abused their new-found freedoms, claiming they had been set free to live as they wished. One can imagine that perhaps women and slaves were those most guilty of this, as they experienced real freedom for the first time in their lives. With all the rules and regulations, one can see a growing concern in the New Testament for the reputation of the church in the world: Dress like this. Wear your hair like this. Say this. Do that. Whatever you say or do, give the world no reason to falsely accuse us. This legalism seemed necessary to the leaders of the church because, eventually, the very survival of the church was at stake.

Finally the young church said, "There are some things we cannot afford to do at this time." The time was not right for women to enjoy their full freedom in Christ. The world at large better understood clear and comfortable distinctions between the different levels of society. Paul asked the women in the early church to submit themselves to their husbands in such a way that the world could approve, or at least have no reason to accuse falsely. It was probably no accident that the phrase in Galatians in which Paul speaks of the distinction between male and female no longer existing was omitted in Colossians 3:11: "Here there cannot be Greek and Jew, circumcised and uncircumcised, barbarian, Scythian, slave, freeman, but Christ is all, and in all." Paul would ask the woman in this letter, as he would in other letters, to voluntarily submit herself to her husband. This was not the time or place to speak of equality.

Though it is true that the wider world closed in on the church in such a way that giving women full freedom within the church became impossible at that time, it is also important to consider that the different books of the New Testament grew out of different communities of faith. In our world we find that there is no universal theology of the woman. In some countries, women are given more freedom within the church than in others. Women are freer in certain churches regardless of location. "It just depends," we say. So it was with the New Testament churches. The overall New Testament picture is one of a great deal of freedom for the women within the churches to exercise their gifts.

The New Testament gives women a precedent for all the roles in our churches in which women hope to participate. Did women teach? Priscilla certainly did. It is important to note that the writer of 1 Timothy says the women of whom he spoke did not teach at the time. It seems they had in the past, however. Some scholars think that the women of this church may have taught heresy. We have no reason to think that this writer intended to be understood as saying that no woman could ever teach. We see in the book of Revelation, written much later, that a woman had been teaching (2:20). John, the writer of the book, had nothing against females teaching, but criticized this woman for teaching lies. Women, nor men, have the option to teach whatever they wish; they must teach the truth.

Did women serve as deacons? Phoebe, whom we meet in Romans 16:1-2, was obviously a woman deacon. Most scholars believe that Junias is a woman's name. Junias is referred to as an apostle in Romans 16:7.

Did women preach? The New Testament is full of accounts of women prophesying, which is basically what we mean in our day by preaching—that is, to have a word from God. Not to be missed is the assumption on the part of Peter in Acts 2 that all the people would prophesy when the Spirit came. The coming of the Spirit qualified the person, male or female, to prophesy or preach.

Did women serve as missionaries? Priscilla and Aquila were a husband and wife missionary team. They traveled and worked together.

Numerous examples in the New Testament indicate that women opened their homes to the church as a meeting place. During the times of persecution this would have been dangerous. Acts 22:4 makes it clear that women, as well as men, suffered for their beliefs. Paul said, "I persecuted this Way to the death, binding and delivering to prison both men and woman."

Interpreting the Difficult Passages

If the New Testament truly gives women a precedent to occupy any and all roles within the church, what do we do with the really difficult passages? Doesn't 1 Timothy 3:8-15 indicate that only men can be deacons? Isn't 1 Corinthians 14:34-36 clear enough that women should not speak in the churches? What about 1 Timothy 2:11-15 in which one finds a whole list of restrictions against the woman—learn in silence with all submissiveness, not teach, not have authority over men, keep silent?

We deal with these passages by affirming the biblical ideal of equality of all persons. We see it in the Old Testament; we see it in the life of Jesus; we see it in Paul. This ideal is our guide. We refuse to read all of the Bible by the light of these three passages. Rather, we read these three passages by the light of the whole Bible. We look in the background of the books for some understanding of the times that helps to explain why the writer would have thought it necessary to curtail the freedoms of women at that point. Finally, we say, going back to the hermeneutical tool we discussed earlier, that these passages are not universals, but particulars. They were instructions intended for the people at that time and place and not necessarily intended for all peoples at all times and places.

1 Timothy 3:8-15 deals with the qualifications for those who would be deacons within the church. By interpreting "husband of one wife" to indicate that only

men can be deacons, many churches have in the past and many still do forbid women from holding the office of deacon in the church. We learn a lot about the times of the book of 1 Timothy by paying close attention as we read. Some dispute within the church is evident (6:4). There had been false teaching (6:3). There was great concern to get along with those in authority and live quiet and peaceful lives (2:1-2). Those in control wanted order in the church and peace with the world, and it seems that whatever measures were necessary to bring them about would be employed.

The place of women in the church was severely restricted. Women were not allowed to teach; perhaps some women had been guilty of teaching falsehoods and/or guilty of contributing to the trouble within the church. Women were not to be in authority over men. It stands to reason that the women had been in authority over men or this would have been a non-issue. Women simply were to be quiet. They were even told how to dress and fix their hair. Women were to find their place in the practice of good deeds and in their role as wife and mother.

One is not surprised to see that the rationale for these restrictions is the "inferior by virtue of having being created second" interpretation of Genesis 2; Genesis 1, the words and actions of Jesus, and Paul's ideal in Galatians 3:28 are completely ignored. One is surprised, however, to find the theological argument

that Adam was not deceived—only Eve was deceived
(2:14)—as justification for the restrictions on women.
The writer of Genesis certainly did not intend to say
that Adam was not deceived. In fact, from what we
learn of the sin offerings of the Old Testament, it is a
serious statement to make that Adam was not deceived,
but he sinned anyway. The Old Testament sacrificial
system offered no sacrifice for these sins—sins "of the
high hand." In other words, Adam had no recourse
through which he could ask for God's forgiveness. The
sacrificial system dealt principally with sins of ignor-
ance or of weakness. Those guilty of presumptuous sins,
such as the writer of 1 Timothy describes, had no hope
of finding forgiveness through the sacrificial system.
One wonders if a tradition, now lost to us, might lie
behind 1 Timothy's argument. It is simply impossible to
know. We see, however, that the writer of this book
will go to great lengths to justify his restrictions on
women.

In light of these arguments, how do we understand
the passage that deals with deacons? First, we say that,
even if this passage is talking about the wives of these
particular deacons and not women deacons in general,
women are not prohibited from being deacons in
churches today because of 1 Timothy. There are other
examples of women deacons in the New Testament, so
this passage is particular and not universal. Even the
restrictions placed on women in this book would not
prohibit these women from performing the duties of the

deacon in that day, which were primarily ministering to people's needs.

The "husband of one wife" phrase may be dealing with something else. Although most scholars believe that both Jews and Gentiles were basically monogamous by this time, a man could legally still have more than one wife.[1] No evidence exists, however, that a woman could ever legally have more than one husband. The writer of 1 Timothy addressed men who could have more than one wife; perhaps some men of the early church did. The writer said that the leaders of the church would practice the "one man, one woman, faithful to death" ideal of God, regardless of the world's laws. There would have been no need to spell out that the women deacons could have only one husband, because they were not legally free to have more than one.

The 1 Corinthians 14:34-36 passage is most troublesome. At least in 1 Timothy the restrictions against women are uniform. In Corinthians the passage appears to indicate that in none of the churches were women to speak, while in this same book women prayed and prophesied aloud in the church. In chapter eleven, it appears that Paul approved of women praying and prophesying, as long as their heads were covered; but, in chapter fourteen, he did not approve of them speaking aloud in any of the churches. What was going on?

In *The New Has Come: Emerging Roles Among Southern Baptist Women*, Linda McKinnish Bridges has a fascinating chapter called "Silencing the Corinthian Men, Not the Women." Bridges points out that reconciling 14:34-36 with the very real fact that women spoke aloud in this very church is not the only problem involved in trying to give a satisfying interpretation of 14:34-36.[2]

Another problem is that the location of the passage is not uniform in the various manuscripts. In some manuscripts, the passage is found after 14:40, in others after verse 33, and in one manuscript in the margin after verse 33. It may be that the copier of that particular manuscript noticed, like countless other readers, that verses 34-36 seem to break Paul's train of thought in chapter 14. They simply seem to be out of place.

To complicate the problem further, Paul's words in verse 36 were addressed only to men. This makes no sense at all given that the women were being called down (vv. 34-35). Also, the author notes, the Greek term for "to be permitted" is found only in 14:34 and 16:7, and in 1 Timothy 2:12. It is impossible to know whether the word was a part of Paul's vocabulary or whether it might have been a borrowed term.

Bridges gives three possible interpretations. One possibility is to accept the text at face value, while trying to reconcile as many of the accompanying problems as possible. For instance, what do we say about single or divorced women, or women whose husbands would not be capable of teaching them at home? Why would Paul use an argument from the law? To which law did he refer? What do we do with the women who prayed and prophesied a couple of chapters back? Why does the text read in such a disjointed way?

Another interpretation is to say that 14:34-36 is a gloss, slipped into Paul's text at a later time in the history of the church by those who were concerned to curb the freedoms of the women in the church. Perhaps they were also anxious to give support to their actions by being able to appeal to a famous figure of the early church. This is an interpretation that makes many Christians, especially more conservative Christians, a bit nervous. Can we not believe that God was keeping a closer vigil than this, students have asked?

According to Bridges,

> The third option for interpretation is to view verses 34-35 as a part of the Corinthian tradition, a slogan from the legalists, or some literary phrase from the opponents of Paul. In this position Paul quotes the opposing view and then refutes it, a rhetorical method which has precedence in the Corinthian letter.[3]

In other words, verses 34-35 are what the Corinthian men said; verse 36 is Paul's rather scathing reply to them.

In 1:12, Paul quoted what the Corinthian men said: "I belong to Paul" or "I belong to Apollos" or "I belong to Cephas" or "I belong to Christ." Paul answered them in 1:13, "Is Christ divided? Was Paul crucified for you? Or were you baptized in the name of Paul?" Bridges points out other spots in 1 Corinthians in which she believes Paul also used quotes and made replies, including, of course, verses 34-36.

This interpretation does not solve all the problems. The section still reads disjointedly, but it is the best we have. Paul moved back into the "free in Christ" camp, which was his ideal vision for the church. This does not mean that he encouraged the church to live out this ideal at whatever cost. As we know, he asked women voluntarily to forfeit some of their freedom for the good of them all. He did that by asking them to live by the accepted social codes of the day. To these we now turn.

The Domestic Codes
(Eph 5:21-6:9; Col 3:18-4:1; 1 Tim 2:9-15; 6:1-2; Titus 2:1-10; 1 Pet 2:13-3:8)

A student wrote of the domestic codes:

> The New Testament writers, with the introduction of the domestic codes into the structure of the church, are dealing with power. They are addressing those who have power, men and masters; and those who do not have power, women, slaves, and children. The writers are dealing with the use and abuse of power. They are asking each of the

> parties involved to do what is hard: women, slaves, and
> children to live peacefully under the power of another;
> men and masters to relate to those over whom they have
> power as though they did not.

He pointed out that each of the parties involved would need the grace of God to do what he or she was called to do.

The writers of the biblical passages that deal with the domestic codes would surely be distressed over some modern-day interpretations of these passages— for instance, interpretations that teach that the needs and desires of the husband and father always come first in the family or that he has the right to make all the decisions within the family and interpretations that give the man the idea that the woman exists solely to fulfill his needs, to clean his house, to care for his children, and to enable him to get ahead in his career. If the woman is unhappy that she has no say in the decisions that directly affect her life, that is her problem. She must pray to God to break her spirit, to make her more submissive.

Some interpretations teach that the child is to be submissive to the parent, even to the extent that child abuse is justified. Some churches tell battered women and children that they are obligated to remain with the abusive husband and father because of his God-given right to rule over them. We must ask ourselves what concept of God is taught by this kind of base interpretation of scripture.

We have covered earlier the background of the New Testament to show why, finally, the early church felt that—perhaps even to survive—it was necessary to curtail some of the freedoms of some of its members. We have shown that women and slaves, the last to gain freedom, were the first to lose it. The church did not invent these codes or orders of society. These were the accepted social structures of the day. The church did ask women and slaves to live by them voluntarily.

We must not try to explain away the domestic codes of the New Testament times, but rather should try to understand them for what they were and then ask what they mean to us. We must not assume that we know what submitting to a husband's authority in that day meant. According to the New Testament, women obviously continued to have important roles to play, within some churches at least, even after the structures of the family within society became the structure of the family within the church. We see from the book of Revelation, for instance, that women must have continued to teach and prophesy. It seems obvious that women continued to open their homes for meeting places for the churches.

It is important to note that Paul and the others called for the willing subordination of the woman to her husband—not to every man, not even to every man within the church. Neither did they call for submission to a husband regardless of his husbandly qualities. The woman was be submissive to a husband who loved her with the same self-sacrificing love that Christ has for the church. It is somewhat hard to imagine that this kind of man would not take her needs and the needs of the family into consideration even though he may have made the important family decisions. We see that children and slaves were instructed to obey; nowhere in the New Testament does one find the wife instructed to *obey* the husband. It seems safe to rule out, then, that submission in that day was, or even included, childlike obedience.

Finally, we consider the significance of the domestic codes for our marriage and family relationships today. Are we to understand, because these codes appear in the Bible, that we cannot as married couples work toward equality in our marriages? Must we order our lives in such a way that the man has the say and the woman and children live with the consequences? Are we obligated to do this? Is it God's will? Would it be sinful to envision and strive for a family structure in which all the members' needs are taken into account?

The answer is, obviously, that we have the right, even the responsibility, to live before God as equals in all of our human relationships. If we need a biblical precedent, we have it in Genesis 1:26-27 and in the words of Jesus concerning equality in marriage. We have also the ideal vision and understanding of Paul in

Galatians 3:28. These passages that contain the domestic codes are to be interpreted as particular. They filled a need in that day, for those people. We are no more obligated to order our marriages by them than we are obligated to keep the dietary laws of the Old Testament. We have the freedom in Christ to live as equals in marriage; we have the responsibility under Christ to consider the needs and desires of our spouses as seriously as we do our own. It is unreasonable to think that everyone's needs can be met at one time. The most pressing needs come first, regardless of the sex of the person with the need.

What about Ordination?

If God has called a woman to a job that requires ordination, then she should be ordained. Nothing in the Bible prevents a woman from ordination; neither does the Bible promote it. The writers of the New Testament simply did not view ordination as we do. Basically what we see in the Bible is the recognition that a person possessed certain gifts that were necessary to do a needed job. The church commissioned that person by the laying on of hands, at that time, for that task. Lifelong ordination with accompanying tax breaks were not part of the biblical milieu. It can be hoped that women might, rather than simply struggle to receive ordination as we practice it, lead the church to rethink the entire process.

Notes

[1]See Bob Adam's unpublished paper, "Jewish Ethics During the Intertestamental Period," (1966) 44, citing Emil Schürer, *A History of the Jewish People in the Times of Jesus* (New York: Schocken, 1961) 151, 350.

[2]Linda McKinnish Bridges, "Silencing the Corinthian Men, Not the Women: An Exegesis of 1 Corinthians 14:34-36." in *The New Has Come: Emerging Roles Among Southern Baptist Women*, ed. Anne Thomas Neil and Virginia Garrett Neely (Washington D.C.: Southern Baptist Alliance, 1989) 41.

[3]Ibid., 44.

Conclusion

We have said that the Bible taken as a whole presents us with an ideal: full equality for each and every person born on the face of the earth. We are equals because we are made in the image of God. Although the structures of society and the structures of language for both Old and New Testaments were almost totally male oriented, the ideal of full equality manages to shine through. We see it in Genesis; we see it in the Old Testament prophets; we see it in the Wisdom literature; we see it in the life of Jesus; we see it in Paul. The early church found it impossible to live out the full freedoms implicit in the gospel. The refrain of the church throughout history has been the same: This is not the time. As women, we ask the church: "Is now the time? If not, why not?"

The church must urgently attempt to incorporate into its life and structures full freedoms for women now, because we are—finally—in the paradoxical situation of women having more freedom, more place, more acceptance outside the church than in it. We have given the world a reason to judge us rather harshly and find us wanting. Something is wrong when basically the world, and not the church, has taken on the task of speaking on behalf of millions of destitute women and children in the world today.

The beautiful thing about the church's relationship with God is that it is never frozen at any point. If we sin, God forgives us. We start again. Just because the church has not been able to accomplish the task before does not mean it cannot be done. God will help us. When we women ask you, Church, "Is now the time?" Say, "Yes, with God's help, yes."